W9-CBM-550

To _____

From _____

First Aid
for the Spirit

Written and compiled by
Sarah M. Hupp

Illustrated by Egidio Antonaccio

Illustrations by Egidio Antonaccio,
Copyright © 1999 and Licensed by
Art Licensing Properties, L.L.C.,
Reproduced by Bentley House®

Inspire Books is an imprint
of Peter Pauper Press, Inc.

For permissions please see
the last page of this book.

Text copyright © 2000
Peter Pauper Press, Inc.
202 Mamaroneck Avenue
White Plains, NY 10601
All rights reserved
ISBN 0-88088-142-9
Printed in China
10   9   8

Visit us at www.peterpauper.com

First Aid
for the
Spirit

Introduction

Bumps and bruises, cuts and scrapes. They are a part of life. Cuts and scrapes respond to the medicines in the first aid kit, but the bumps and bruises to our lives seem to cut deeper. Where can we go to find help for those sudden injuries of the heart? What can make us feel better?

One answer: God! As we recognize our place in God's plan and learn of our value to Him, encouragement heals our hearts. And as we trust Him to bring good out of every situation, we find the soothing comfort of peace. Let "First Aid for the Spirit" bandage those unexpected hurts or troubles in your life. Center your focus on God and feel better fast!

S. M. H.

Trust God where you cannot trace him. Do not try to penetrate the cloud he brings over you; rather look to the rainbow that is on it. The mystery is God's; the promise is yours.

John Macduff

$\mathcal{T}$he surest mark
of a Christian is not
faith, or even love,
but joy.

Samuel M. Shoemaker

*I*f your life is producing only a whine, instead of the wine, then ruthlessly kick it out. It is definitely a crime for a Christian to be weak in God's strength.

Oswald Chambers

$\mathcal{B}$lessed are you
who weep now,
for you shall laugh.

Luke 6:21 NKJV

*Resolve to keep happy,
and your joy shall form
an invincible host
against difficulty.*

Helen Keller

It often does you
more good to be tested
like this than to have
things always going the
way you want them to.

Thomas à Kempis

*E*very day is a fresh
beginning;
Listen, my soul, to the
glad refrain,
And, spite of old sorrow
and older sinning,
And puzzles forecasted and
possible pain,
Take heart with the day, and
begin again.

Susan Coolidge

*O*ftentimes it's easier
to recognize someone else's
blessings in disguise than it
is to recognize our own.

*N*ever doubt
in the dark what God
told you in the light.

V. Raymond Edman

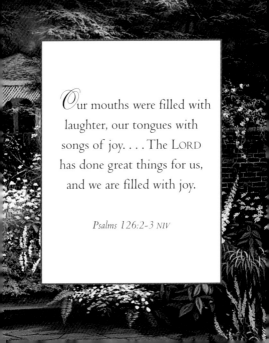

*O*ur mouths were filled with laughter, our tongues with songs of joy. . . . The LORD has done great things for us, and we are filled with joy.

Psalms 126:2-3 NIV

$\mathcal{T}$hose who bring
sunshine into the lives
of others cannot keep
it from themselves.

J. M. Barrie

*K*ind words, spoken
in due season, are God's
bridges of love. . . . Let words
of cheer and praise be the
order of the day . . .

Charles Stanley

God doesn't leave us on
our own. As we wrap our
hands around a task, and in
faith begin to exert force,
eureka! Divine energy
surges through us.

Joni Eareckson Tada

*L*et not your heart

be troubled . . .

John 14:1 KJV

The devil is a chronic grumbler. The Christian ought to be a living doxology.

Martin Luther

Encouragement is one of God's most joyous art forms. . . . Some people combine a helping hand with a word of praise and produce a grateful heart. . . . Belief and support build self-esteem. Persistent prayer composes a song of hope; and tenderness and warm embraces fashion a friend.

Susan Lenzkes

*I*f God waits longer than
you could wish, it is only to
make the blessing doubly
precious! . . . Our times
are in His hands. . . .
He will make haste for
our help, and not delay
one hour too long.

Andrew Murray

*J*esus said: "In this world you will have trouble. But take heart! I have overcome the world."

John 16:33 NIV

*A*dversity is the
diamond dust Heaven
polishes its jewels with.

Robert Leighton

If I stoop
Into a dark tremendous sea
of cloud,
It is but for a time;
I press God's lamp
Close to my breast;
its splendour, soon or late,
Will pierce the gloom:
I shall emerge one day.

Robert Browning

The road of life is
sometimes steep too.
It is a beautiful thing to
have friends who encourage
me by stopping to talk.
It is also beautiful when
I can provide a rest stop
and brighten someone
else's climb.

Sandra Drescher-Lehman

$\mathcal{Y}$ou are my hiding place;
You shall preserve me from
trouble; You shall surround me
with songs of deliverance.

Psalms 32:7 NKJV

$\mathcal{R}$ub your eyes and purify
your heart and prize above all
else in the world those who love
you and wish you well.

Alexander Solzhenitsyn

*[D]*on't pray when
it rains if you don't pray
when the sun shines.

Satchel Paige

*B*ehind the cloud the
starlight lurks,
Through showers the
sunbeams fall;
For God, who loveth
all his works,
Has left his hope for all.

John Greenleaf Whittier

God is my salvation,
I will trust and not be afraid;
for the LORD God is my
strength and song, and
He has become
my salvation.

Isaiah 12:2 NASB

*O*ne doesn't discover
new lands without consenting
to lose sight of the shore
for a very long time.

André Gide

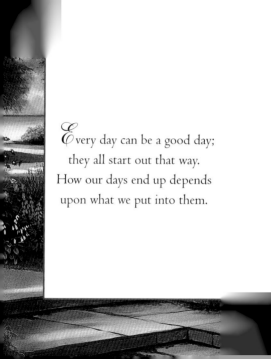

*E*very day can be a good day;
they all start out that way.
How our days end up depends
upon what we put into them.

A kind heart is
a fountain of gladness,
making everything in its
vicinity freshen into smiles.

Washington Irving

$\mathcal{T}$he LORD is good
to those who wait for Him,
to the person who seeks Him.

Lamentations 3:25 NASB

[T]he strong, and the eager—how hard it is for them to wait! . . . [S]uch waiting takes a mighty faith. And yet faith which waits shall surely see. The glory of God comes to the waiting one.

James H. McConkey

*T*here is no burden
so heavy that when lifted
cheerfully with love in our
hearts will not become
a blessing to us.

J. R. Miller

*S*torms never last. The night always gives way to the sunrise. One season always yields to the next. So, too, our human impossibilities become divine miracles. We need only trust and wait.

*E*ncouragement has never filled a flat tire . . . made a car payment . . . nor fixed a broken washing machine. But encouragement from another gives us the strength to do what we feel we cannot do. . . . Encouragement. Doesn't sound like much, but it's everything.

Sharon Mahoe

*T*he tide turns at low water
as well as at high.

H. Havelock Ellis

*[W]*hen I fall, I shall arise;
when I sit in darkness, the
LORD shall be a light unto me.

Micah 7:8 KJV

What cannot be bought, begged, borrowed, or stolen because it has no value unless given away? A smile! Give one away today. It will only take a moment—but all who receive it will be enriched by it.

$\mathscr{T}$he greatest use
of life is to spend it for
something that will outlast it.

William James

*W*hat we are is
more significant, in the long
run, than what we do. It is
impossible for a man to give
what he does not have.

Elton Trueblood

$\mathcal{D}$on't be afraid
to go out on a limb.
That's where the fruit is.

E. C. McKenzie

Only man clogs
his happiness with care,
destroying what is, with
thoughts of what may be.

John Dryden

*L*et this be my crown,
O Lord. I will only triumph in
You once I have learned the
radiance of the rain.

George Matheson

*W*e can trust God because
His word is reliable, His
character is dependable,
His power is inexhaustible. He
will not fail you . . . disappoint
you . . . forsake you . . . ignore
you . . . or forget you!

Roy Lessin

[T]hey that wait upon the LORD shall renew their strength; they shall mount up with wings as eagles; they shall run, and not be weary; and they shall walk, and not faint.

Isaiah 40:31 KJV

*A*lmighty God, Sustainer,
show to us in everything we
touch and in everyone we meet
the continued assurance of thy
presence round us: lest ever we
should think thee absent.

George Macleod

*F*ailure is not a sin.
Faithlessness is.

Henrietta Mears

"*I* shall strengthen them in the L<small>ORD</small>, And in His name they will walk," declares the L<small>ORD</small>.

Zechariah 10:12 <small>NASB</small>

There are souls in this
world which have the gift
of finding joy everywhere
and of leaving it behind
them when they go.

Frederick William Faber

Other men see only a
hopeless end, but the Christian
rejoices in an endless hope.

Gilbert M. Beenken

The future is as bright as
the promises of God.

William Carey

$\mathcal{T}$he LORD is my strength
and my shield; my heart trusted
in him, and I am helped . . .

Psalms 28:7 KJV

*G*od has given each of us
a priceless gift of joy in Jesus.
How easy it is to lose our joy in
the scurrying around of life. Yet
it is always there to find, if we
will but pause and listen to
the beautiful presence of
Jesus in our hearts.

James S. Hewitt

$\mathcal{L}$et no one ever come to you without leaving better and happier. Be the living expression of God's kindness: kindness in your face, kindness in your eyes, kindness in your smile.

Mother Teresa

[*T*]he mountains are
God's thoughts upheaved,
the rivers are God's thoughts
in motion, the oceans are God's
thoughts imbedded, the
dewdrops are God's thoughts
in pearls.

Sam Jones

$\mathcal{A}$ pat on the back, though only a few vertebrae removed from a kick in the pants, is miles ahead in results.

E. C. McKenzie

[*J*]ust as the sufferings of Christ are ours in abundance, so also our comfort is abundant through Christ.

2 Corinthians 1:5 NASB

The wise man seeks little joys, knowing that life is long and that his quota of great joys is distinctly limited.

William Feather

$\mathcal{T}$he hand of faith must lift the gracious gift to the parched lips, and so refresh the panting soul. . . . Stretch out thy "lame hand of faith," and take the holy, hallowing energy offered by the Lord.

J. H. Jowett

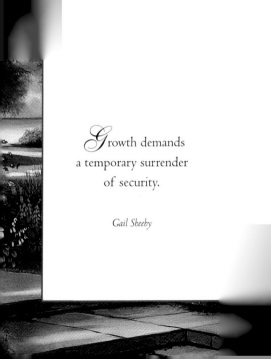

$\mathcal{G}$rowth demands
a temporary surrender
of security.

Gail Sheehy

*A*s your days,
so shall your strength be.

Deuteronomy 33:25 NKJV

*G*od has made me laugh,

and all who hear

will laugh with me.

Genesis 21:6 NKJV

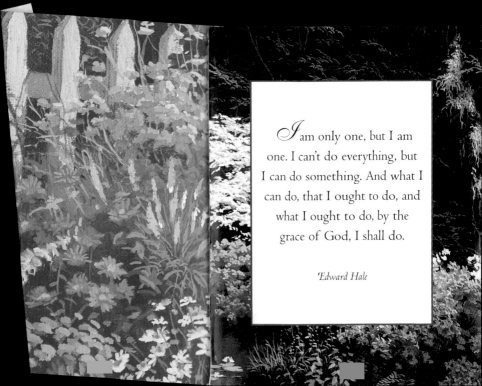

I am only one, but I am one. I can't do everything, but I can do something. And what I can do, that I ought to do, and what I ought to do, by the grace of God, I shall do.

'Edward Hale

I am only one, but I am one. I can't do everything, but I can do something. And what I can do, that I ought to do, and what I ought to do, by the grace of God, I shall do.

'Edward Hale